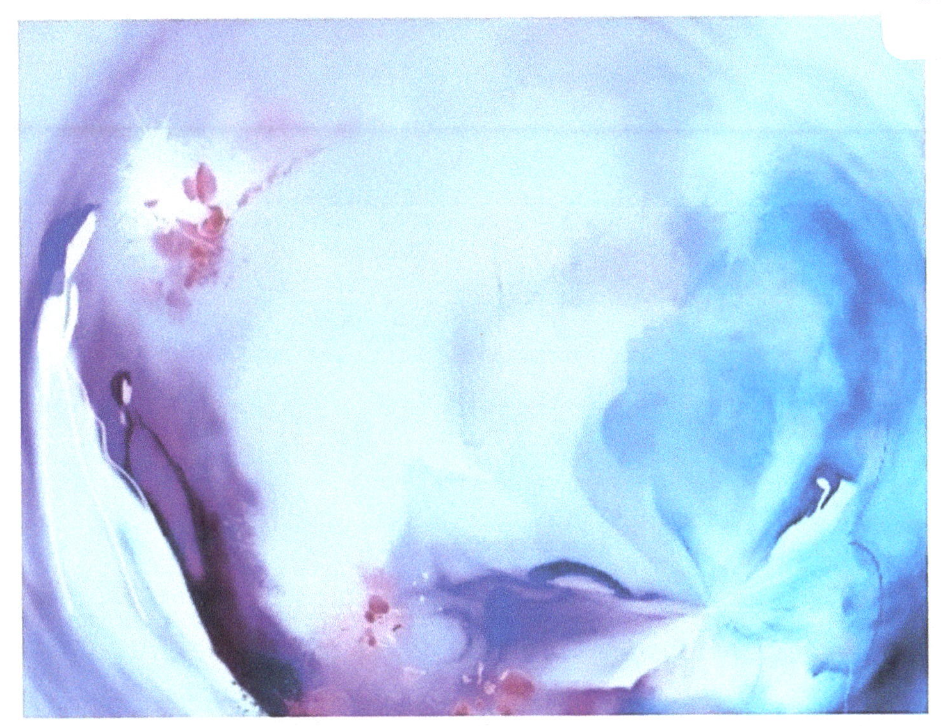

百卉流光，影顏篇

詩與畫　瀾若

Woman with no face

Art and poem　Lan Ruo

在筆觸與色彩交織的歲月里，
感謝大哥與二哥的鼓勵與支持，助我從猶疑中拾回勇氣。
親朋好友與同窗舊識，如林間光影，一路相伴，低語相勉。
特別感謝先生，兩位兒子與好友莉莉，
協助校稿，猶如春日柔風，溫暖心田。
這部詩畫集，
是我獻給世界的一縷感恩與溫情。

○

Through the years where brushstrokes and colors have intertwined,
I am deeply grateful to my eldest and second brothers for their encouragement and
support,
helping me reclaim my courage from moments of doubt.

To dear relatives, friends, and classmates from days past—
You have been like shifting light and shadow in the forest,
walking beside me, offering quiet words of encouragement.

A special thanks to my husband Steve, my sons Kiliii, Alexander, and my dear friend
Lili,
whose help in proofreading was like the gentle spring breeze
That warms the heart.

This collection of poetry and paintings is a small thread of gratitude
I offer to the world, woven from affection and light.

詩，是靈魂的低語；
畫，是心境的留影。

作者簡介
瀾若，本名顏世蓮 ，生於台灣大甲，自幼喜愛繪畫，中學時獲台北市長獎。
赴美後曾於格林霧圖書館舉辦畫展，後入藥學院與醫學院，
執業行醫多年。閒暇時筆墨不輟，
以詩與畫寄託對生命的熱愛與對世界的溫情

Poetry is the whisper of the soul;
Painting is the lingering image of the heart.

Author's Biography
Lan Ruo, born Dianna Yan in Taipei, discovered her love for
painting at an early age, earning the Taipei Mayor's Award
in high school. After moving to the United States, she
presented a solo exhibition at the Glenwood Library before
embarking on studies in both pharmacy and medicine. For
many years, she devoted herself to the art of healing, yet
in the quiet spaces of life, her brush and pen have never
been still—offering through poetry and painting a tender
tribute to life, and a gentle embrace for the world.

創作者的感悟：百卉流光・影顏篇

“百卉流光・影顏篇” 是一方想象的天地——每位女性都可以是任何人，卻不被限定。
有的畫作有雙眼，悄然邀你共鳴；有的則保持神秘，靜默而開放。
存在與缺失、可見與不可見之間，這組作品翩翩起舞——畫與詩的交響，
邀請你去發現那張面孔之外，璀璨的靈魂。

Artist's Reflection: The Woman with No Face

The Woman with No Face is a space for imagination, where every
woman can be anyone, yet no one is defined. Some portraits
hold eyes, a quiet invitation to connect; others keep their
mystery, silent and open.
Between presence and absence, seen and unseen, this collection
dances, a poem in paint and verse, inviting you to discover the
luminous soul beyond the face.

目錄 - Table of Contents

百卉流光　·　序

在花影與流光之間，她用畫筆描摹女子的身姿，

用詩句傾聽生命的呼吸。

——致一位婦產科醫師的詩意凝視

當一位日日迎接新生命的醫者執起畫筆，那些從診間流淌出來的女性故事，便化作宣紙上盛放的第二次分娩。

《百卉流光》四十五首詩與畫，是醫者的眼，也是女子的心——溫柔、堅韌、閃著光。它同時是一則關於「影顏篇」的故事——那些沒有被五官和外貌框住的女子，在色彩與詩行中，展現獨一無二的生命形象。她們的容顏，或許不在畫中；她們的氣韻，卻在每一筆色彩、每一行詩句裡流動。

第一章 · 自然的低語——女性，作為生命最初的隱喻。

在〈石畔雲慰〉中，斜倚的線條呼應骨盆孕育的弧度；〈採秋圖〉里，原野與低垂的樹，與婦女的腰線共享著豐收的節奏。最令人動容的，是〈青銅雕深深動〉：當冰冷的醫療器械化作古老的青銅紋飾，我們才讀懂——那些被視作脆弱的曲線，正是人類文明的承重柱。

第二章 · 她自世界來——力量與韌性的詩意側影。

〈獨立自信新女性〉的潑彩下，藏著剖腹產疤痕後的從容；〈來自非洲謎一樣的女人〉，用赭紅堆疊出子宮內膜的厚度。這些畫作並非歌頌"偉大"，而是如〈碧水泛游〉般淡定，呈現女性在疼痛與勇氣間自我渡航的本能。

第三章 · 詩中女子，畫中情懷——人生與情感的低聲絮語。

〈盼麟兒〉的留白，是孕晚期那份緊張而甜蜜的等待；〈雙人舞〉飄動的衣袂，彷彿是胎心監護儀上跳躍的線。產房簾幕後，那些最貼近生命的語言，正在被一針一線地織成花冠。

第四章 · 鏡中詩行——的自拍詩畫，恰似超聲影像上的自我凝視。

在〈秋韻〉中，她以豐盈的秋色渲染自己的心靈；〈舞興盈盈滿素裙〉，無聲卻盛滿喜悅；〈擁抱生命的詩篇〉中，接生婆之於新生兒，不過是見證了原本就存在的生命光芒。

整部《百卉流光》，是一場溫柔的"文學與醫術的縫合"——用詩句為未被言說的美與善打結，用色彩為生命導回柔軟的居所。

或許，這本書最深的診斷，藏在〈雨潤春光〉那抹水墨的細縫里：

所有關於女性的藝術，最終都在回答一個問題——

我們，是凝望花的人，還是本身就是被凝望的花？而「影顏篇」提醒我們，答案不必寫在臉上。

——是為序

俞國基

07/31/2025

俞國基，國際報人，曾任台灣時報、台灣日報、中國時報、聯合版、民報、美國北美日報總編輯以及自由時報副社長。也曾任職故宮博物院中國美術史研究院。

The Woman With No Face - Preface

Between the shadows of flowers and the flowing light,

she paints the posture of women with her brush

and listens to the breath of life through her verses.

—To an obstetrician's poetic gaze.

When a physician who welcomes new life every day takes up a paintbrush, the women's stories that flow from the consultation room blossom a second time upon the rice paper.

The Woman with No Face, truly a Luminous Blossom — forty-five poems and paintings — is the physician's eyes, and also a woman's heart: gentle, resilient, and luminous.

It is also a story about The Hidden Radiance—women who are not confined by features or appearances, yet reveal their unique life essence through color and verse.

Their faces may not appear in the paintings.

Their spirit flows in every stroke of color, every line of poetry.

Chapter One · Nature's Whisper — Woman as the first metaphor of life.

In Resting Clouds by the Stone, reclining lines echo the curves of the pelvis that nurture life; in Gathering Autumn, the fields and the drooping trees share the same rhythm of harvest as a woman's waistline. Most moving of all is The Deep Motion of Bronze Sculpture: when cold medical instruments are transformed into ancient bronze motifs, we understand—those curves once thought fragile are, in truth, the load-bearing pillars of human civilization.

Chapter Two · She Comes from the World — A poetic profile of strength and endurance.

Beneath the washes of color in The Independent and Confident New Woman lies the composure after a caesarean scar; in The Enigmatic Woman from Africa, ochre-red layers suggest the thickness of the endometrium. These paintings do not glorify "greatness" — rather, like Drifting on Blue Waters, they calmly portray a woman's instinct to navigate herself between pain and courage.

Chapter Three · The Woman in Poetry, the Sentiment in Painting — Quiet murmurings of life and emotion.

The blank spaces in Awaiting the Unicorn Child hold the tense yet sweet anticipation of late pregnancy; the flowing garments in Pas de Deux resemble the leaping lines on a fetal heart monitor. Behind the curtain of the delivery room, the language closest to life is being woven, stitch by stitch, into a crown of flowers.

Chapter Four · Verses in the Mirror — Self-portraits in poetry and painting, like gazing at oneself in an ultrasound image.

In Autumn Charm, she bathes her soul in the abundance of autumn hues; in Dancing Gracefully in a Flowing Skirt, there is no sound, yet joy overflows; in An Embrace to Life's Poem, the midwife, to the newborn, is merely a witness to the light of life that was already there.

The entire Woman with no Face is a tender "suturing" of literature and medicine—tying knots in verse for beauties and kindnesses unspoken, guiding life back to a soft dwelling through color.

Perhaps the book's deepest diagnosis lies in the fine seams of ink in Spring Light after the Rain:

All art about women ultimately answers a single question—

Are we the ones gazing at the flowers, or are we ourselves the flowers being gazed upon?

And The Woman with No Face reminds us: the answer need not be written on the face.

— Written as the Preface

Yu, Kuo-Chi

July 31, 2025

Yu, Kuo-chi — International journalist, former editor-in-chief of Taiwan Times, Taiwan Daily, China Times, United News, The Independent Evening Post, and The North America Daily in the United States, and former deputy publisher of The Liberty Times. Also served at the National Palace Museum's Institute of Chinese Art History.

第一章　自然的低語
Whisper of Nature

1-1　雨閏春光

雨潤春光

〜〜瀾若

春雨清飄逸

隨風潛世間

山林漸次醒

芽瓣綻藍天

Springlight Bathed in Rain

~ ~Lan Ruo

Spring rain drifts light, serene

With wind, it slips unseen

The woods awake, refreshed, alive

And buds reach blue skies to thrive.

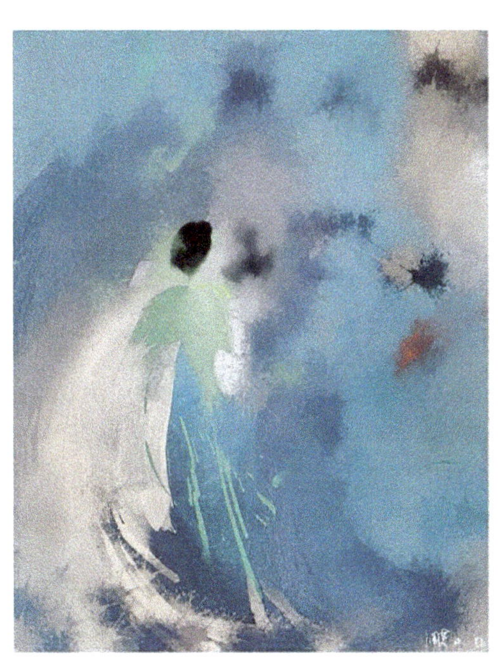

石畔云憩

〜〜瀾若

素裳落石影，鬢散半遮腮
腰柳因風軟，眸心向晚開
衣垂青靄染，夢與流雲裁
不著傾城色，天風送韻來

Resting by the Stone Bench, Among Clouds

~ ~Lan Ruo

In plain robe on the oblong bench, she sits so still
Her hair half-veiled, soft shadows brush her cheek
The willow-waist sways with the breeze's will
While twilight wakes the heart of the eyes, unique

Her sleeves drip down, steeped in haze's dye
Her dreams shear clouds that drift past hill to hill
No need for hues to make the crowd cry
Heaven's wind hums the rhyme no art could speak.

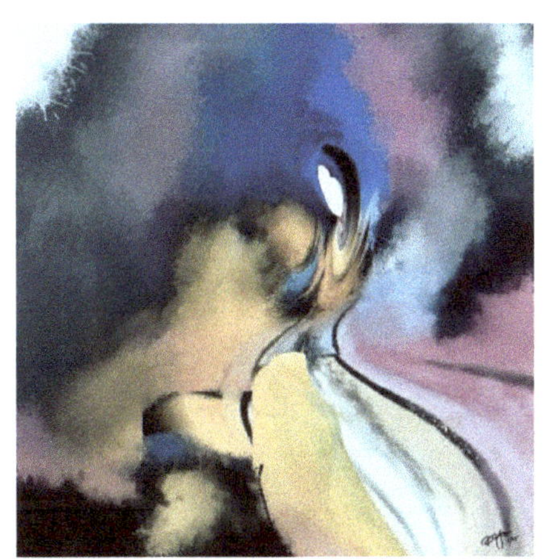

採秋圖

〜〜瀾若

碧草接穹蒼，
金楓點淡妝。
偶然拾錦色，
籃滿貯晴光。

An Autumn Gathering

~ ~Lan Ruo

The emerald grass stretches to meet the sky
Golden maples blush with a gentle dye.
By chance, she gathers hues of splendor bright
Her basket brims with sunlight's tender light.

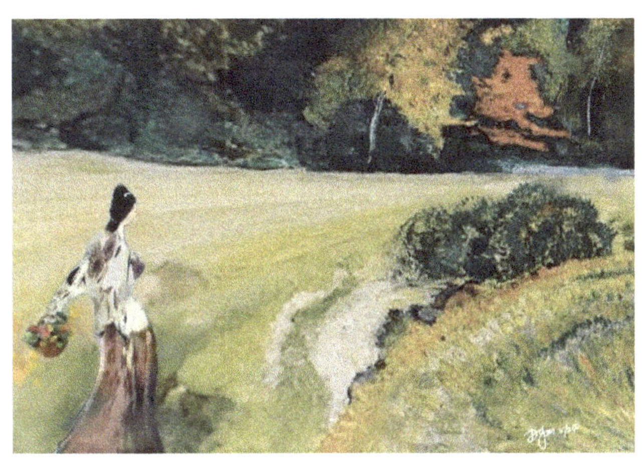

青铜雕深深動

〜〜瀾若

素身無飾立蒼茫
靜氣初觀只尋常
忽覺弧光涵太初
為伊坐到月生涼

Bronze Carving's Profound Stir

~ ~Lan Ruo

Unadorned, it stands in vastness bare

At first glance, nothing rare

Till a primal gleam arcs through the air

For it, I sit till moonlight chills my chai.

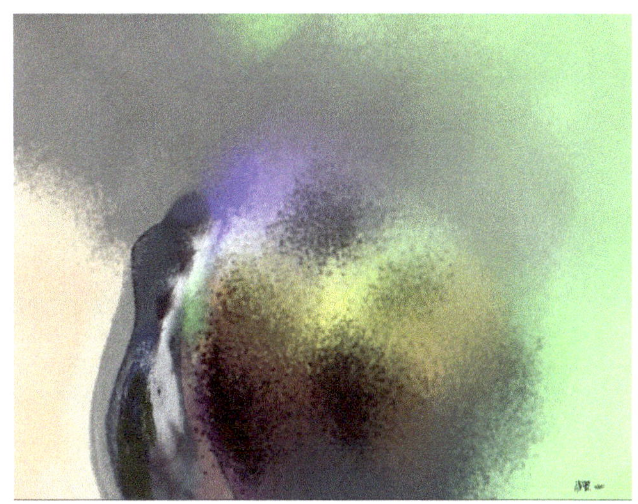

仙姿吟

～～瀾若

曉拂香塵繞砌行
花間霧散見綃輕
翩然疑是瑤台客
一步春風一履馨

Ode to a Celestial Grace

～～Lan Ruo

Dawn's perfumed dust hugs the garden's stone

Through parting mist—a silk-draped form blown.

Immortal from jade halls above

Each step wakes spring, each breath perfumes the grove.

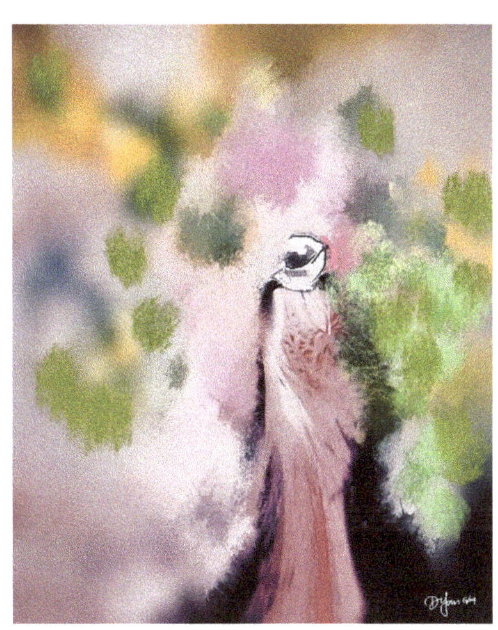

翠蔭裙影
～～瀾若

綠蔭遮陽爽
幽幽碧草柔
百花爭艷舞
輕裙蝶影悠

Shade of Green, Silken Grace

~ ~Lan Ruo

Lush shade shields from summer's gleam
Soft grass whispers in a dream
Blossoms dance in colors bright
Silk skirts drift like butterflies' flight.

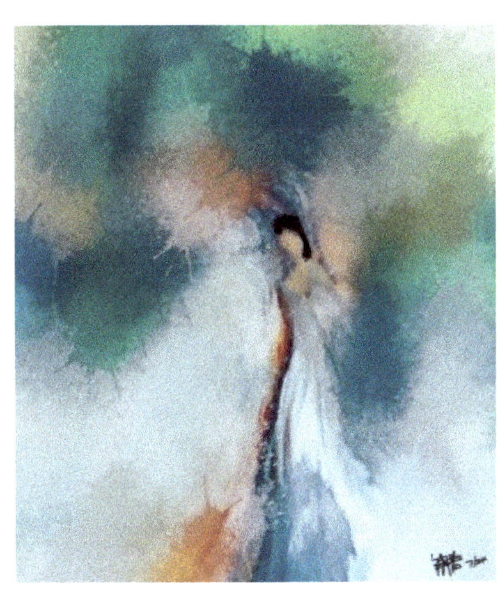

秋丘望遠

～～瀾若

秋丘人獨步
遠望入蒼煙
萬里歸心寄
蒼茫一念牽

Autumn Hill, Looking Afar

~ ~Lan Ruo

I walk alone upon the autumn hill,
Where vision drifts into the fading haze.
My heart, though scattered miles away,
It is gently bound by autumn's endless breath.

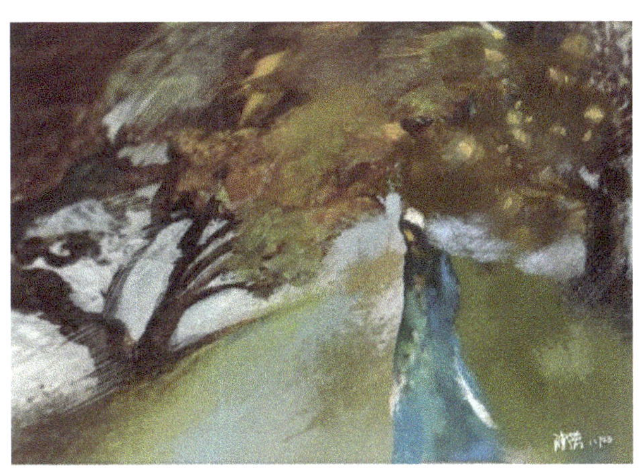

蒼穹藍渺

～～瀾若

極北寒空舞藍暉
旋光炫影照天涯
幽然幻境何曾識
雪落銀川共彩華

Vast Azure Firmament

~ ~Lan Ruo

In polar skies, blue arcs unfurl.
Spiraling radiance gleams and swirls
Who has glimpsed this mystic sight
As snow-clad, glow in light.

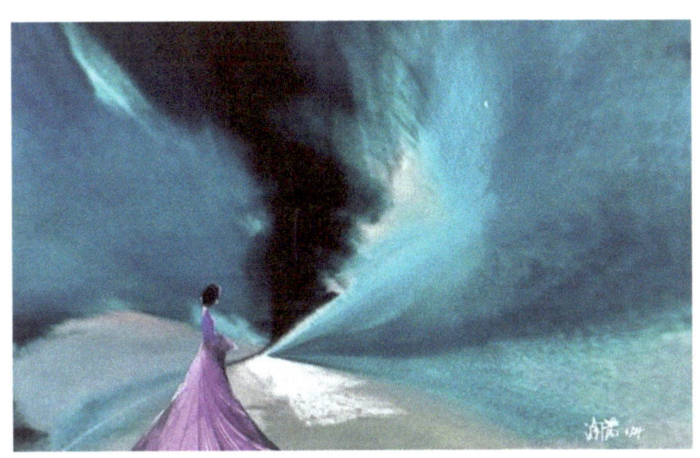

第一章　自然的低語

1- 秋日小園嘻相邀

秋日小園嘻相邀

～～瀾若

三姝倚坐石磴邊
笑語輕盈繞小園
不染脂香秋色裡
風生玉影自生妍

Autumn Garden, A Playful Invitation

~ ~Lan Ruo

Three maidens rest by mossy stone steps
Their laughter dances through the garden air
No rouge adorns their autumn-kissed grace
The breeze stirs beauty, light as silken flare.

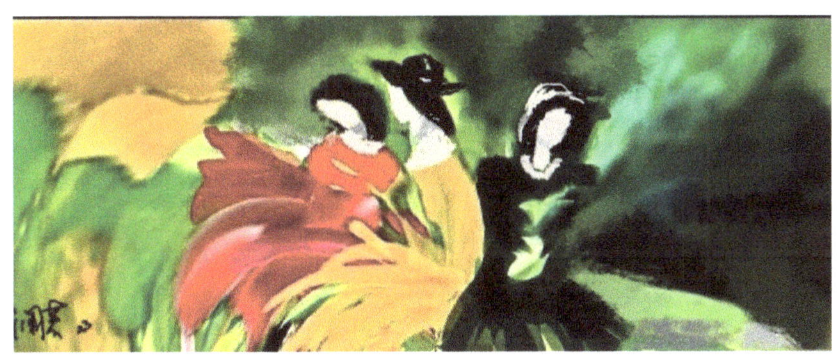

古韓景吟
〜〜瀾若

長裳立翠丘
寺影映碧流
微風搖松影
海色入晴眸

Ancient Korea: A Scene

~ ~Lan Ruo

She stands upon the emerald hill,
Temple shadows drifting over blue.
Pines ripple gently in the breeze,
The sea's light caught in her gaze.

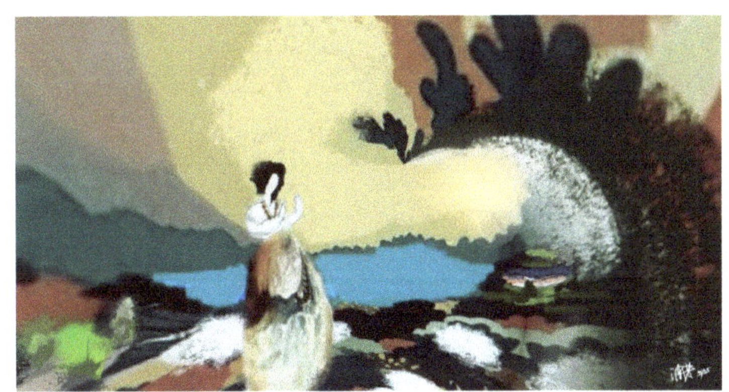

閒看美京華府春色
〜〜瀾若

微雨美京潤如絲
枝頭新綠尚難知
最宜心緒初回暖
閒看煙光漸入詩

Leisurely Gazing at Spring in D.C.

~ ~Lan Ruo

A gentle rain through Washington flows like a thread
New green on boughs, half-seen and half-unsaid
Best when the heart first stirs from winter's dream
While drifting, mists slip softly into the poem and stream.

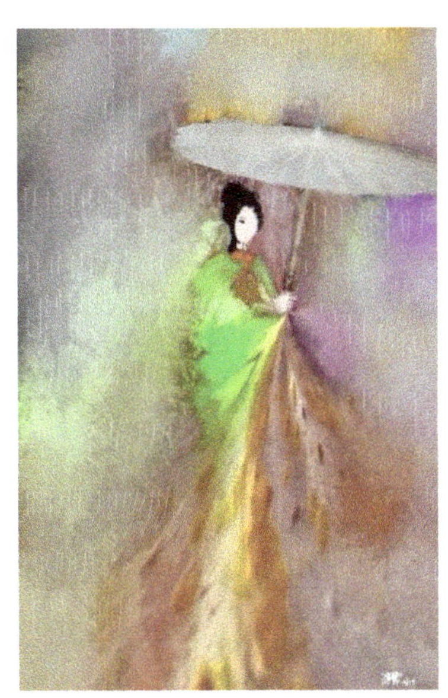

晨興

～～瀾若

雨洗晨光淡，風攜野草香
遠山蒙薄霧，近水覺新涼
踩石驚魚影，聽松忘路長
心隨雲去處，天地即吾鄉

Roaming the Wild

~ ~ Lan Ruo

Morning light rinsed pale by rain
Wind carries wild grass'sweet refrain
Distant hills in mist arrayed
Fresh chill off the stream is laid

Stepping stones stir fish—a flash
Pines hum, the long path's forgotten
My heart drifts where clouds may roam
The world becomes my only home.

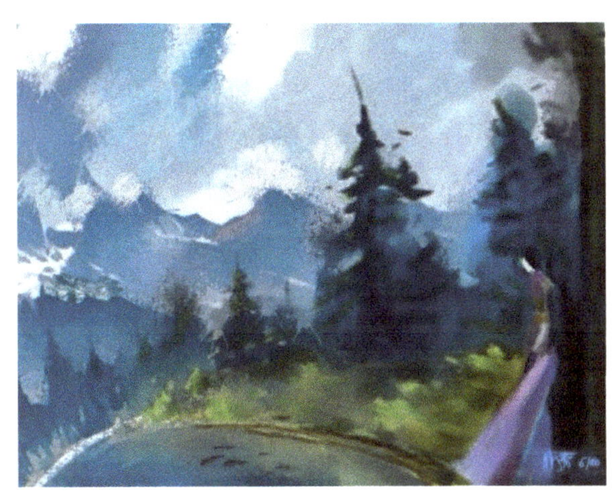

山行

～～瀾若

青山綠蔭漫，空翠濕人衣
風拂面親處，濛濛心神飛
欲問投簪處，前溪有鹿蹤

Mountain Stroll

~ ~Lan Ruo

Emerald peaks, a canopy of shade so wide

The air's green mist dampens my robe's side

Where the breeze strokes my face, tender and light

My spirit soars through hazy delight

To ask where to lay my pin and rest一

A deer's tracks mark the stream's path west.

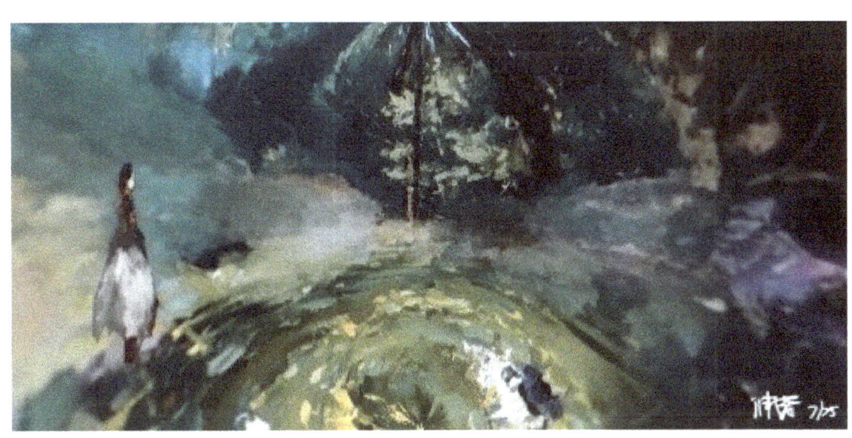

幽芳晨漫

〜〜瀾若

晨曦照庭園，微風拂葉旋
繁英迎露笑，幽馥繞身嫣
霞影流光潤，幽芳染步沿
芳華雖燦爛，素心最悠然

Fragrant Dawn's Embrace

~ ~Lan Ruo

Morning light graces the blooms,
Gentle winds dance through the room.
Flowers greet the dawn with cheer,
Fragrance lingers soft and near.
Radiant hues in misty air,
Silent scents along the stairs.
Though blossoms gleam in vivid hue,
A quiet heart finds joy most true.

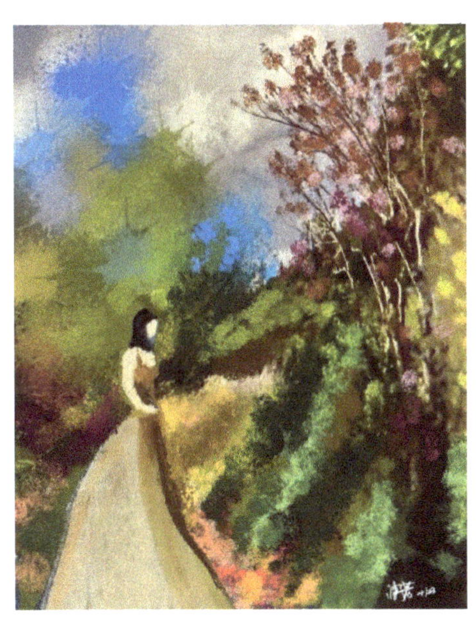

獨立自信新女性

～～瀾若

心光照朝日，笑意逐東風
筆起描雲夢，髮飛龍嘯中
眉藏明月色，眼映萬山空
信步無懼路，乘帆向遠空

Independent Woman

~ ~ Lan Ruo

She Moves Like Morning

She glows—not with fire, but with something gentler

like sunlight spilled across the floor

Her laughter finds the wind and dances with it

brief and brilliant

She paints in dreams, in silks and stardust

her voice part tide, part thunder

The moon has touched her brow

The mountains sleep in her gaze

She walks on—barefoot and certain

toward whatever calls her name.

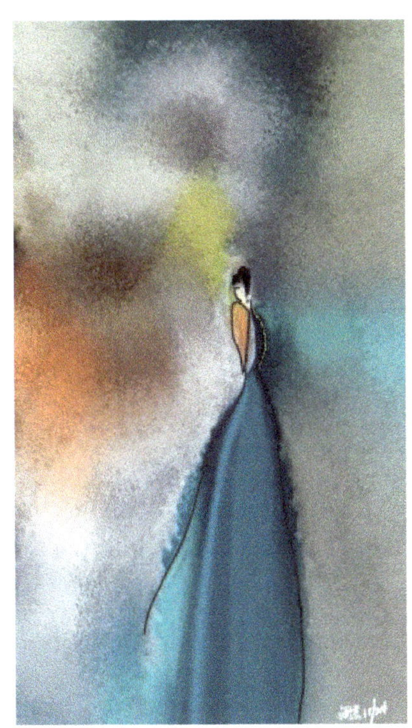

丹青韵玉眸

〜〜瀾若

碧袖飄搖倩影柔
霞光點染玉顏幽
人間難繪真妍色
唯有丹青寫玉眸

Graceful Eyes in Painted Hues

~ ~ LanRuo

The painted lilt of jade eyes

Her emerald sleeves sway in gentle grace

A blush of dawn gilds her tranquil face

No brush on earth can shape such true allure

Save for art's hand to trace her jade-bright gaze.

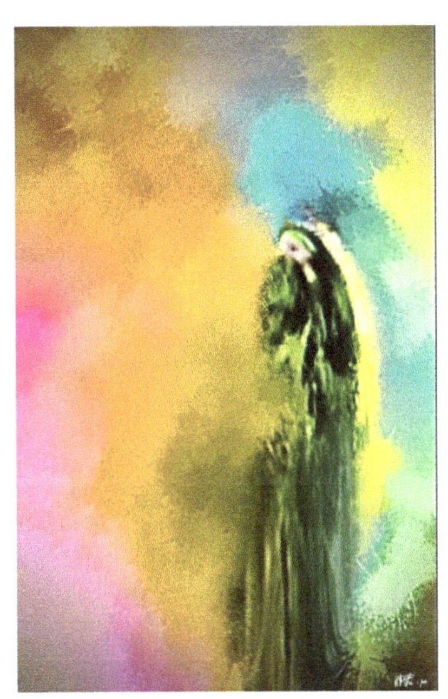

非洲佳人
〜〜瀾若

黑膚映日光，
衣彩任風揚。
髮帶隨風飛，
眸中星影長。

African Beauty

~ ~ Lan Ruo

Her dark skin glows beneath the sun,
Vivid robes drifting with the breeze.
A hairband lifts with playful wind,
Stars linger in her watching eyes.

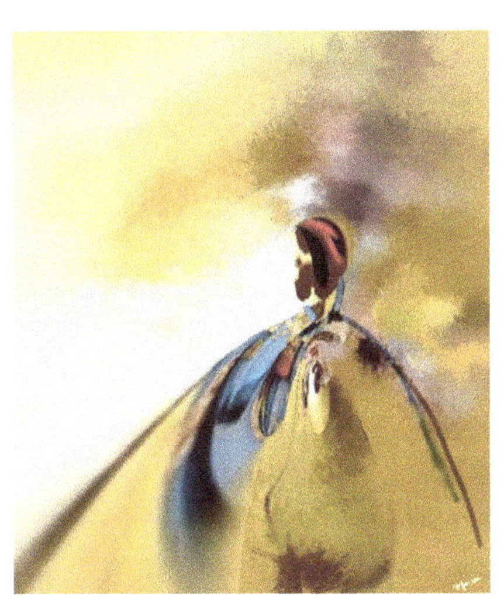

西班牙一瞥
～～瀾若

西女慢行夕日斜
微风轻拂鬈絲尖
心随浪漫吉他曲
野草芬芳葡酒甜

A Glimpse of Spain

~ ~Lan Ruo

A Spanish maiden strolls in dusk's embrace
The breeze caresses locks with tender grace
Her heart beats with the guitar's soulful song
Wine, sweet and wild blooms drift scents along.

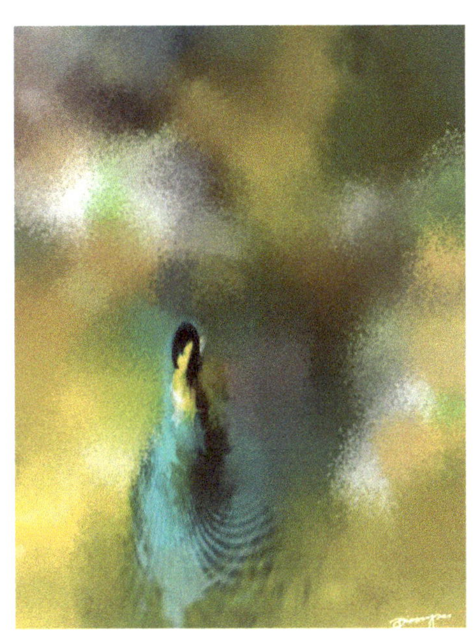

海地女翩然

～～澜若

海地女翩然，随歌鼓韵传
裙扬云影舞，袖展花颜鲜
姿婉随清调，步轻溪语绵
忘情游舞境，尘虑尽云烟

The Haitian Elegance Unfolding

~ ~ Lan Ruo

The Haitian maiden, graceful and free
Moves to the rhythm of the drum and melody
Her skirt sways like dancing clouds on high
Her sleeves unfold, fresh as blossoms nigh
Her form sways with the purest tune
Her steps light as a babbling brook's croon
Lost in the realm of dance, her spirit takes flight
All worldly worries vanish in the soft moonlight

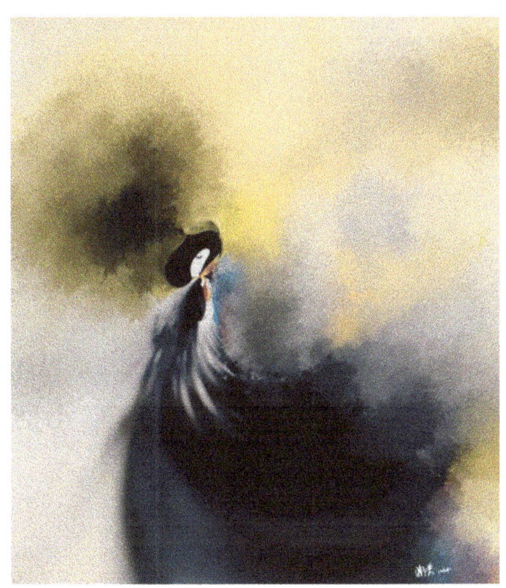

丹麥佳麗－依拉

〜〜瀾若

丹麥有佳麗

端然且淡泊

性情嫻雅靜

愁寄意難托

Beauty Fair In Denmark

~ ~Lan Ruo

Denmark has a beauty fair

Graceful, modest, pure of air

Gentle, quiet, kind at heart

Yet sorrow lingers, love departs.

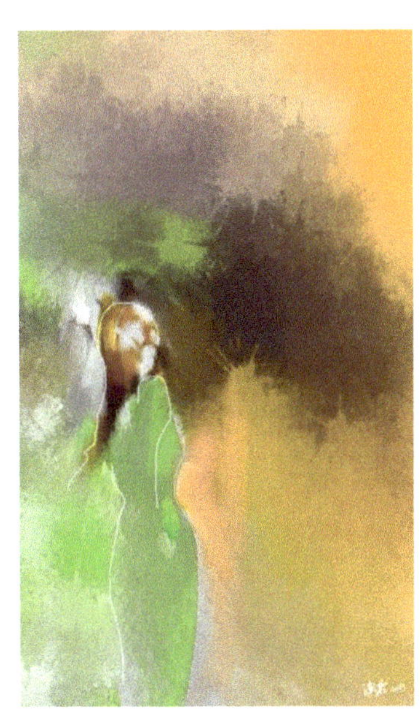

窈窕淑女
～～瀾若

背影窈窕曳長裙
步搖輕轉氣韻芬
回眸一笑群芳黯
照破凡心入夢魂

Mademoiselle

~ ~Lan Ruo

Her silhouette glides in a flowing dress
Each step exudes a charm no words can express
One smile she turns, all flowers lose their glow
She stirs the hearts, where dreams and passions grow.

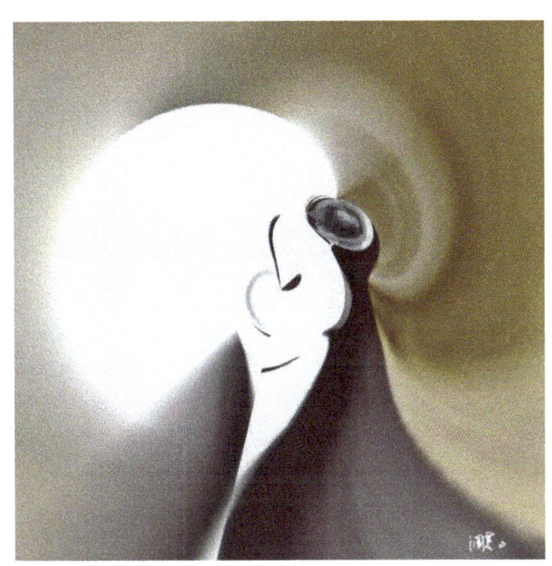

碧水泛舟・東方佳人
～～瀾若

輕盈小艇泛青波
素裹紅妝映綠蘿
水面漣漪光弄影
風輕花笑醉烟渦

Drifting on Emerald Waters- Beauty of the East

~ ~Lan Ruo

A light boat drifts on emerald waves so clear
In simple hues, red accents softly appear
Ripples dance as fish play with their shade
Breeze whispers, flowers laugh in the mist's cascade.

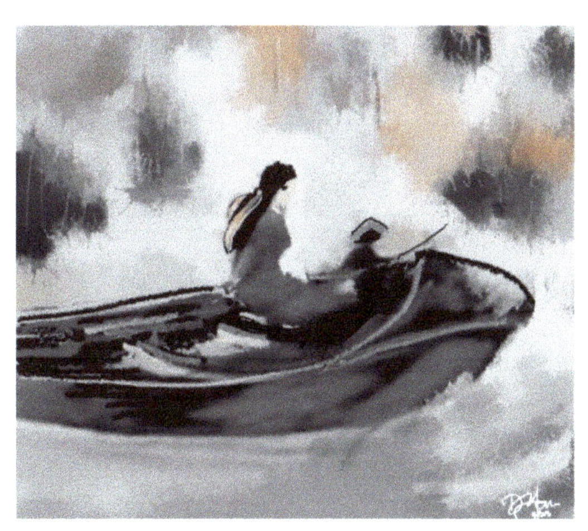

妙齡

〜〜瀾若

青絲隨風舞
輕步夢中尋
晨曦融笑靨
云影映羅襟
幽思添韻色
芳齡映夢痕

Radiant Youth

~ ~Lan Ruo

Silken strands in breezes flow

Soft steps chase dreams aglow

Dawnlight warms her beaming face

Clouds drift by in misty grace

Thoughts weave hues both bright and true

Youth glows where dream winds blow.

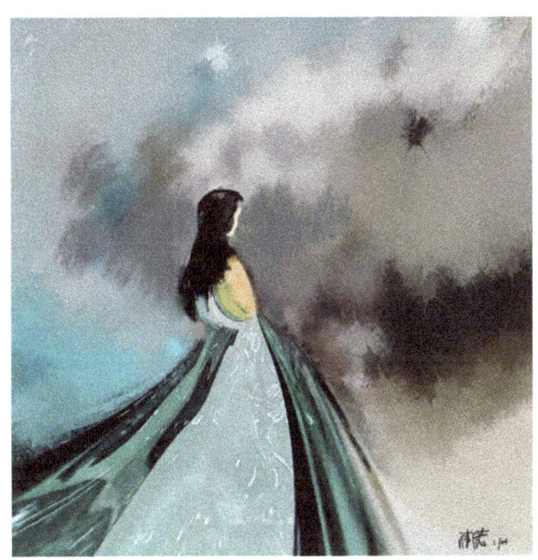

愛琴海的幻影

〜〜瀾若

輕紗掩玉姿
月隱雅容依
女神風裁影
仙歌畫里迷
煙波如舊色
眉眼訴幽思

Phantom of the Aegean Sea

~ ~Lan Ruo

Veiled in silk, her jade form glows
Moonlight hides where beauty flows
A goddess' touch in drifting shade
Divine songs whisper, softly laid
Mist-bound waves in hues remain
Eyes reflect a deep refrain.

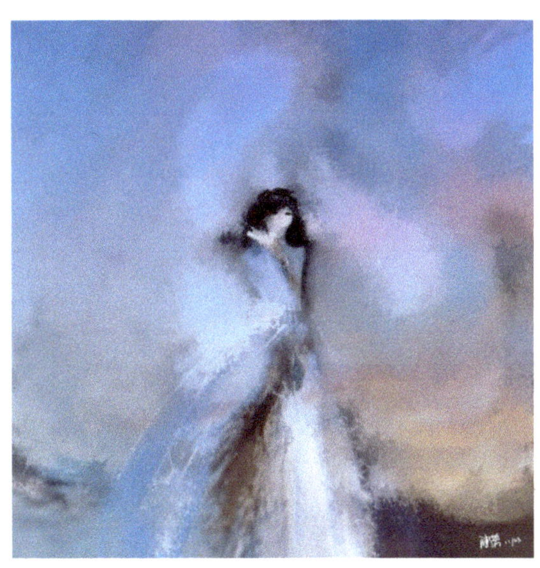

匈牙利村姑吟

～～瀾若

清婉村姑勤樸素
趕集割麥伴晨曦
春風吹面雨絲細
輕步吟歌陌上怡

Song of the Village Maiden

~ ~Lan Ruo

Soft-spoken maiden, humble and bright

She wakes with the fields and walks toward the light

Spring wind caresses, rain beads her brow

She sings on the footpath, gentle and low.

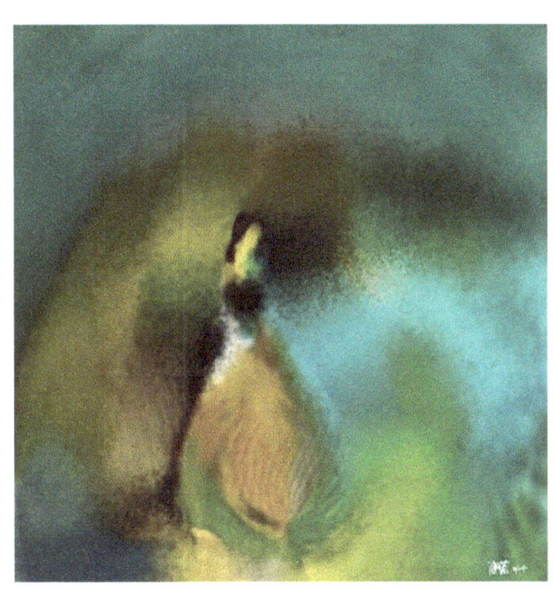

第三章　詩中女子，畫中情懷。
Verses of Her, Strokes of Feeling

3-1　夢中倩影入畫中

夢中倩影入畫中
～～瀾若

不染塵華心謐靜
無憂歲月笑相隨
夢中倩影如詩幻
筆抹浮形入畫扉

A Graceful Vision, Dreamt into Form

~ ~Lan Ruo

Untouched by dust, the heart stays still

With laughter, carefree years fulfill

A fleeting dream, a vision fair

A brushstroke paints her presence there

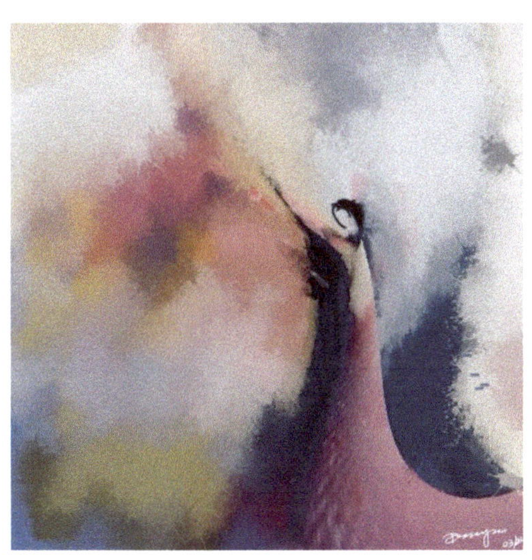

神怡

〜〜瀾若

霓裳雙袖挽
飄然若雲撫
如雪從風散
流光影中舞

Serene Grace

~ ~Lan Ruo

Melody stirs silk in flight

Steps unfold with measured light

Spinning—scattering a thousand snows

Drunkenly embracing fleeting shadows' glow.

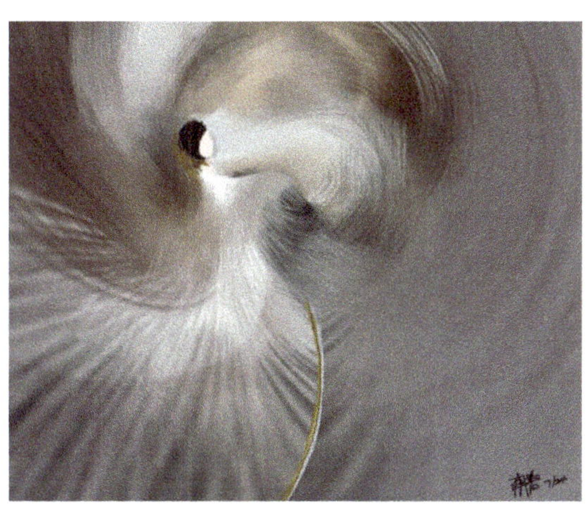

憂鬱

〜〜瀾若

深院冷爐寂
孤身緊鎖眉
袖濕淒楚在
何處可除哀

Melancholy

~ ~Lan Ruo

Cold hearth in a silent hall

Alone, she locks her brows in pain

Sleeves damp with sorrow's call

Where can one dispel disdain.

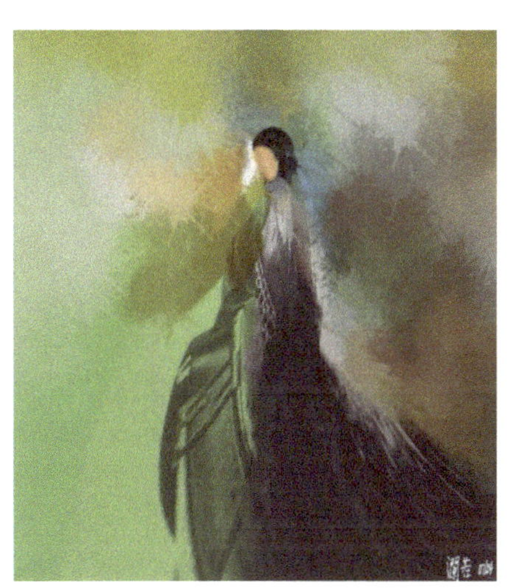

雙舞
〜〜瀾若

晚宴佳餚罄交歡
歌揚美韻舞翩跹
長衫輕擺衣裙转
曼妙疏狂漾心間

Dual Dance

~ ~ Lan Ruo

The feast dissolves in shared delight

As songs take flight, as one they sway

Silken robes spin, skirts bloom bright—

My heart drifts in passion's glow.

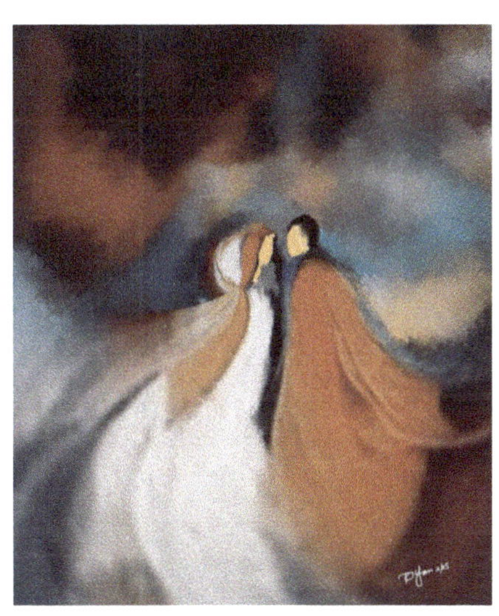

月夜錦書
～～瀾若

庭靜香浮桂影疏
素娥凝立月華初
新箋未展情難掩
細讀書中舊夢餘

Moonlit Letter

~ ~Lan Ruo

The courtyard breathes with cassia's trailing scent
She stands alone, in moonlight, softly bent
The page unopened, yet her heart takes flight
Old dreams awaken in the silver light.

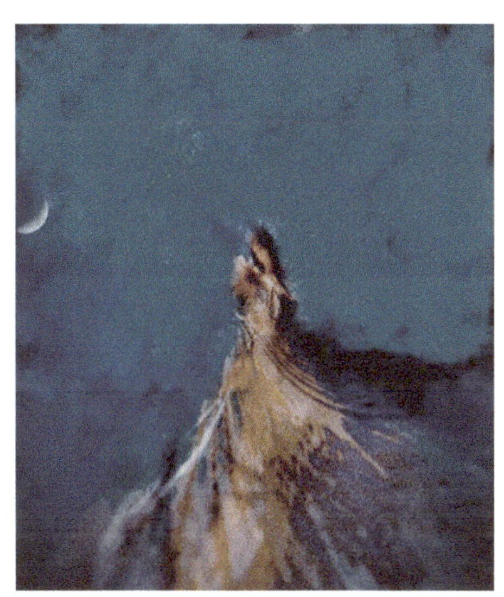

畫裏芳華

～～瀾若

畫里芳姿難掩映
繪中倩影總流連
誰言背影無顏色
氣度風華勝萬千

Elegance in Art

~ ~Lan Ruo

Her elegance in the painting, impossible to conceal

Her enchanting figure lingers, a vision surreal

Who says a silhouette lacks color or hue

Her grace and charm outshine countless views.

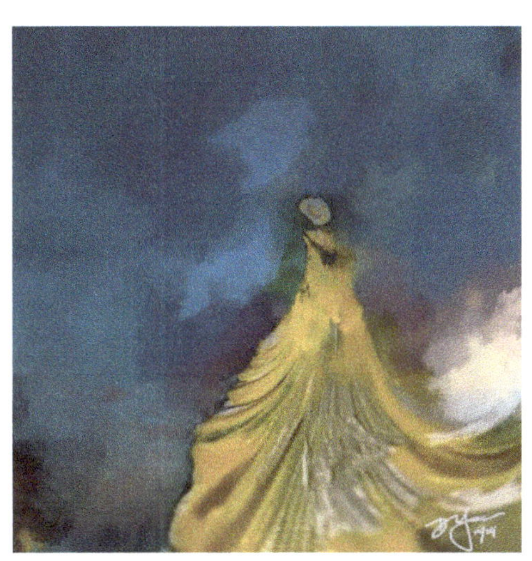

3-7 娉婷少女

娉婷少女

〜〜瀾若

飄然輕步迎風立
閒適隨心自懶姿
娉婷初苞羞且澀
誰人不念少年時

Graceful and Shy

~ ~Lan Ruo

With gentle steps, she meets the breeze

At ease, her form a tranquil tease

In tender bloom, she hides her face

Who wouldn't recall youth's fleeting grace

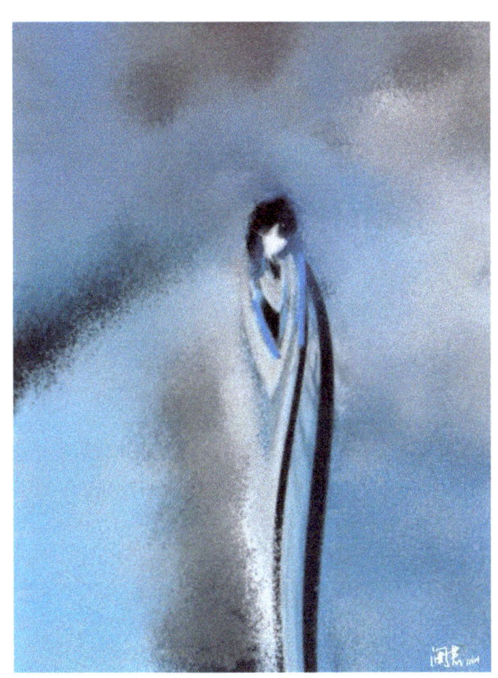

櫻花淚-蝴蝶夫人（觀 DC 櫻花有感）

～～瀾若

白宮春雲軟，	東瀛舊夢廻
嬌花凝露顫，	風雨碎枝裁
瓣落无人扫，	痴心恨未埋
芳魂銷匕首，	帶淚問櫻埃

Tears of the Sakura – Madame Butterfly

~ ~Lan Ruo

Soft spring clouds above the White House glide
Twining old vines from the Eastern tide
Blushing blooms tremble with morning dew
Wind and rain cut branches clean in two

Petals fall, uncared for on the ground—
Love unmet, yet still in longing bound.
Fragrant soul consumed by dagger's will,
With tears, she questions cherry ashes still.

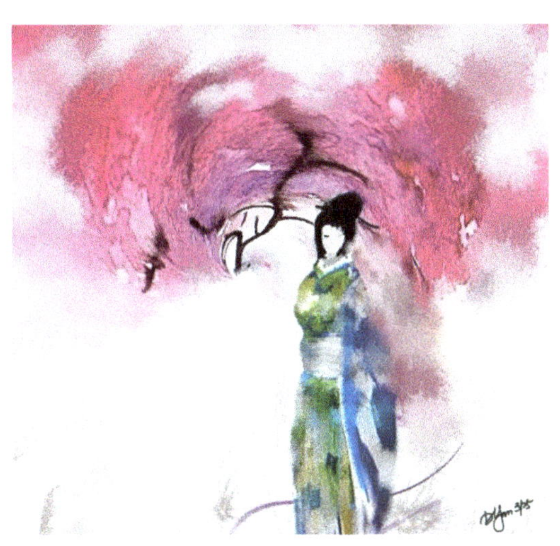

雲間詩旅

〜〜瀾若

我欲穿花尋詩路
直飛雲朵覓仙鄉
身隨嵐麓踏幽徑
手攬白虹御風翔

Chasing Dreams on Clouds

~ ~ LanRuo

I seek the path through blossoms bright
To trace the clouds in realms of light
My steps ascend where mists unfold
My hands embrace the rainbow's hold.

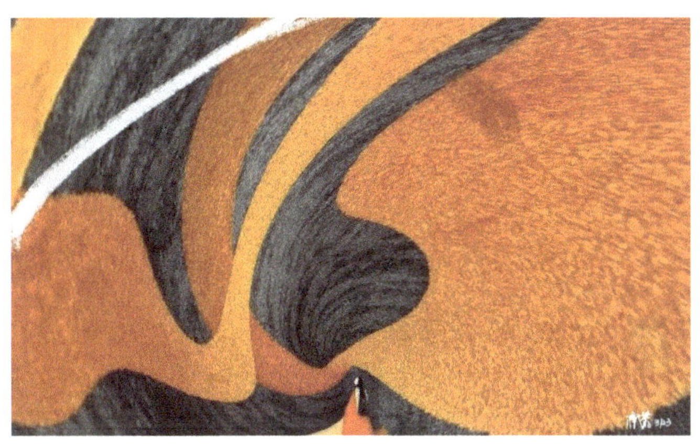

圓窗影閒

～～瀾若

圓窗開靜界
坐望雲無邊
身安塵外境
心遠世間緣

Tranquil Silhouettes

~ ~Lan Ruo

The round window frames the still domain

She sits and watches the boundless cloud

At peace beyond the dust of life

Her heart untraced by the worldly crowd.

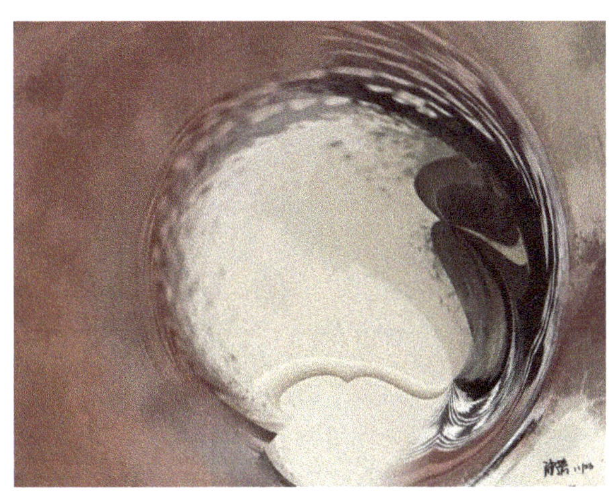

茶花女

～～瀾若

紅燭照憔悴
輕煙寄夢懷
浮生皆幻影
淚落逐花開

Camellia Dream

~ ~ Lan Ruo

The red candle lights despair
Soft smoke carries dreams away
Life is but a fleeting glare
Tears fall where flowers sway.

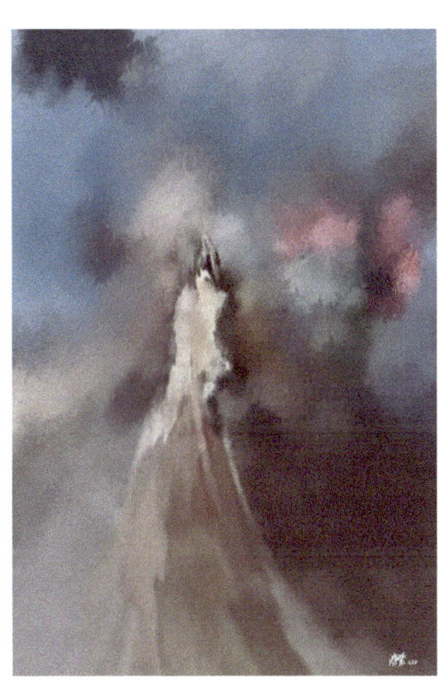

娘懷

～～瀾若

世有一方隅
柔堅兩不渝
窄寬皆是愛
恆依母懷余

A Mother's Bosom

~ ~Lan Ruo

There exists a sacred space,
Tender yet steadfast, beyond erase.
Narrow or vast—all love embraces,
Forever cradled in her soft grace.

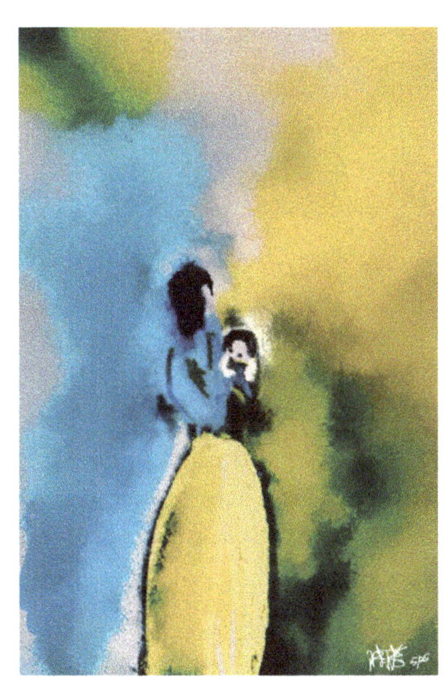

宴春光

～～瀾若

晨曦霞影明
行歌伴落英
欲行花牽袂
回首春滿襟

Spring Fills My Heart

~ ~ Lan Ruo

Morning glow, bright as dawn,
Songs accompany falling blossoms.
Flowers cling as I take my leave,
Turning back—spring fills my heart.

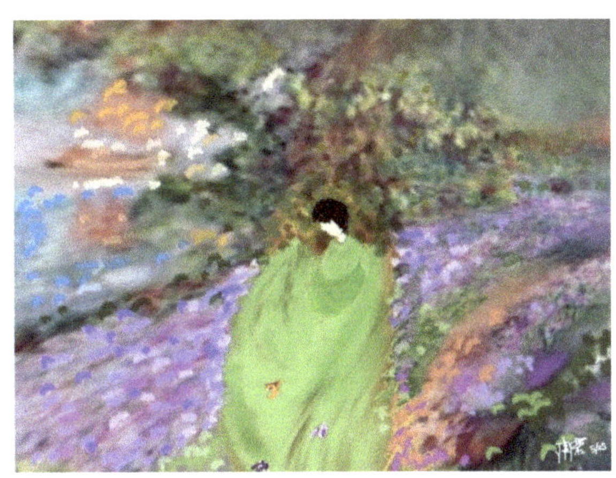

陌上清風
～～瀾若

疏立原野靜
遙瞻陌花菲
香隨野風遠
素袂帶雲歸

Clear Breeze Over Paths

~ ~ Lan Ruo

Stands alone in the tranquil field
gazing afar at fading blooms
Fragrance drifts with wandering winds
white sleeves trail the clouds home.

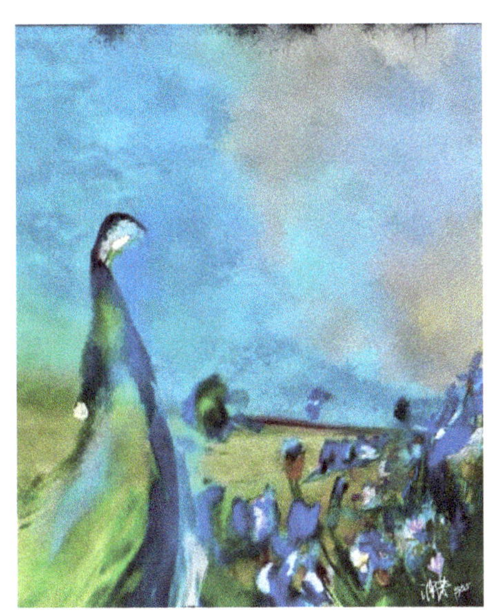

露華

〜〜瀾若

翩翩不及姿
香馥勝花枝
雲過輕拂面
心隨影夢馳

Radiant Dew

~ ~Lan Ruo

Grace outshines the swallows' flight

Fragrance richer than blooming boughs

Clouds drift by, a touch so light—

My heart follows dreams, her shadow allows.

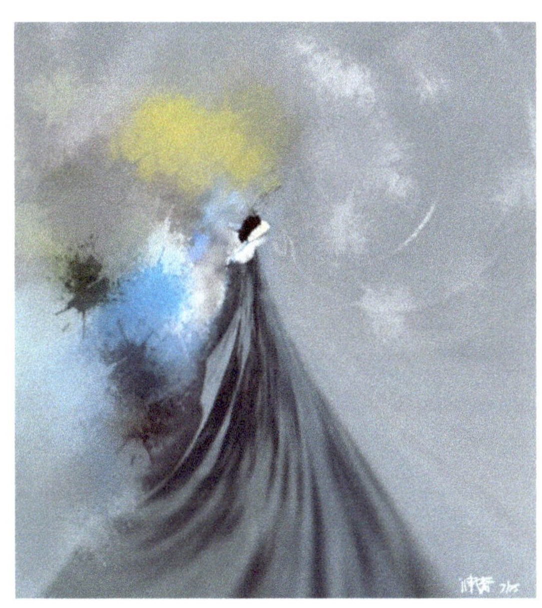

畫外之畫
～～瀾若

畫前藍衣立
心融筆無痕
靜賞成新作
形合映墨痕
誰言身外客
意境本為人

Beyond the Painted Veil

~ ~Lan Ruo

Before the art, she stands in blue

her thoughts dissolve where brush runs clear

In quiet awe, a work is born

her form absorbed in ink's soft mirror

Is she but an outside soul

The scene exists because she's near.

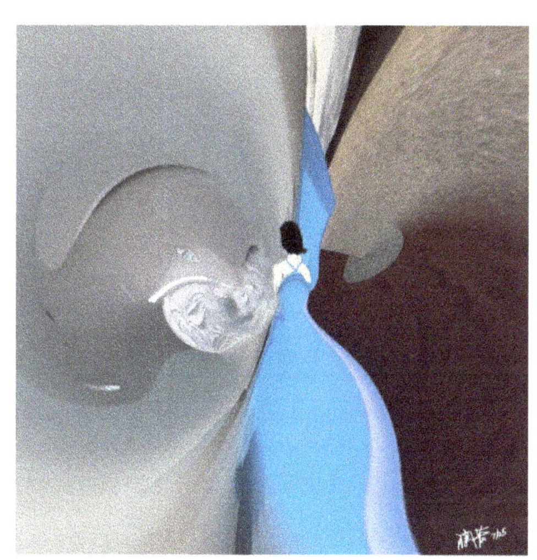

怡然
〜〜瀾若

綠柳白梨屏
紅櫻伴露台
晨光煦暖意
獨坐愛貓偎

Tranquil in Terrace

~ ~Lan Ruo

White pear and willow form a leafy screen
Red cherries gleam where morning dew has been
The sun drapes warmth across the waking day
Alone I sit, my cat curled close to stay.

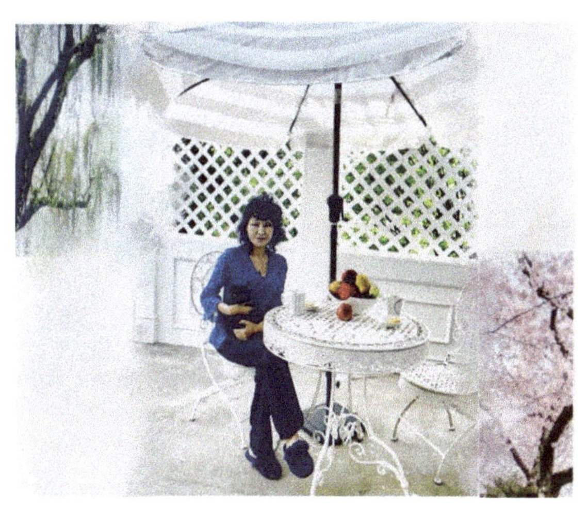

秋韻
〜〜瀾若

葉喧楓漫舞
林動滿襟秋
裊裊佳人立
幽幽清素留

Autumn's Melody

~ ~Lan Ruo

The maples dance, their leaves sing low

The woods breathe autumn, soft and slow

There stands a maid, so pure, so bright

A wistful grace, a lingering light

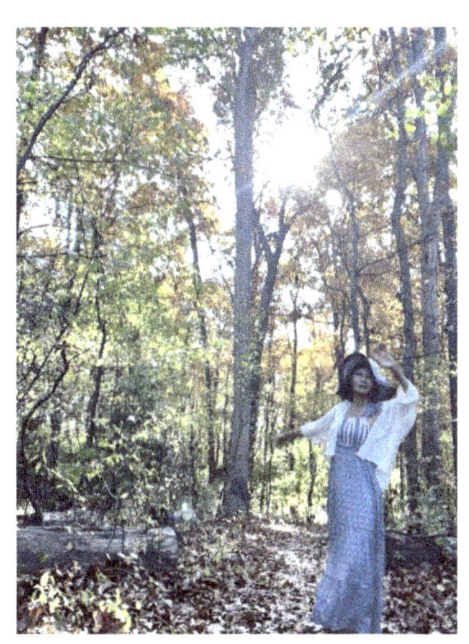

冬霧倉韻
～～瀾若

細雪如絲霧織茵
槎枝放拂影輕輪
倉暖承冬融霧繭
天賜地欣養物淳

Elegance of Winter Mist and Barn

~ ~Lan Ruo

Threads of snow weave mist on emerald leaves
On rugged boughs, shadows waltz gracefully
The barn holds winter, cradling fog's embrace
Earth and heavens nurture life's gentle grace.

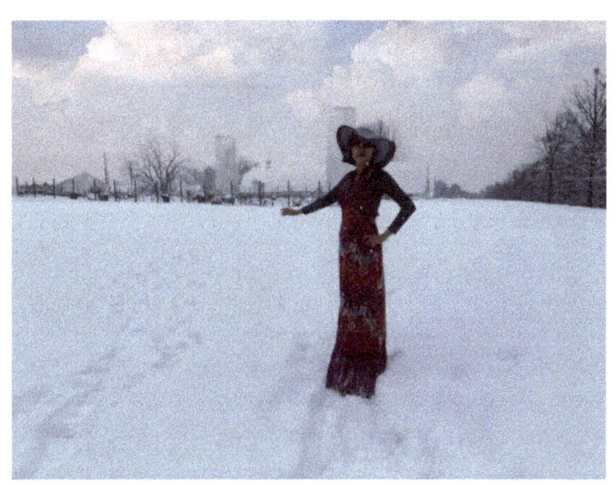

舞興盈盈滿羅裙
～～瀾若

晨曦和煦挾云手
薄霧清柔豁我心
門外獨徉千翠圃
盈盈舞興滿羅裙

Dancing with Joy

~ ~ Lan Ruo

The morning sun clasps clouds in tender play
Soft mist dissolves my cares and clears the way
Through emerald fields I roam beyond the gate
My flowing skirt caught in a dancing state.

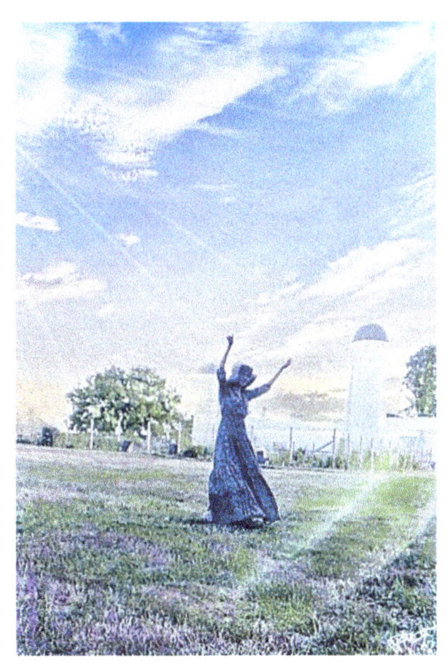

擁報生命的詩篇
〜〜瀾若

生命如花映碧霄，
靈魂似葉舞雲裳
隨緣風雨天地闊，
情寄山川自飄芳。

An Ode to Embracing Life

~ ~Lan Ruo

Life blooms like flowers in azure skies,
The soul dances as leaves in clouds arise.
Through wind and rain, the world expands wide,
Affection flows where mountains reside.

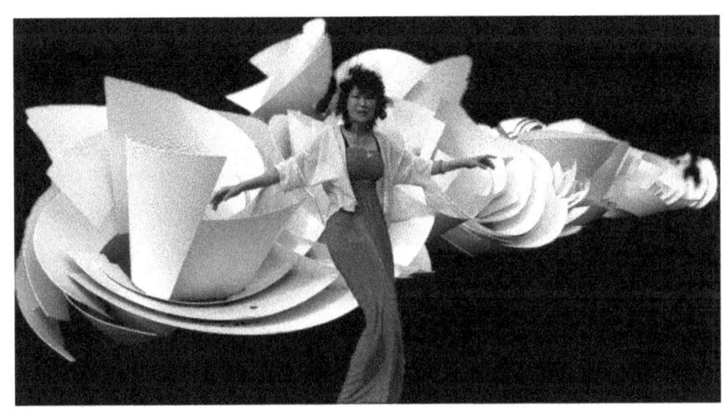

書尾結語

歲月如詩，光陰如畫。
這四十五首詩與畫，彷彿是靜夜裡的低語，心靈
深處的光影交織。
每一行詩句，都是一次與自我的對話。每一幅畫作，
都是心靈的顯影。

在創作的過程中，我在字裡行間尋找自由，也在色彩流動中體會生命的韻律。
我漸漸明白，「影顏篇」並不是一個沒有面孔的人，而是每一位不被外貌定義的女子──她的容顏，存在
於她的故事與氣息中。

願這些詩與畫，能在您的心湖泛起微光，帶來片刻的寧靜與共鳴。
感謝您，願意陪伴我走過這段創作的旅程。

Afterword

Time flows like poetry, and moments unfold like paintings.
These 45 poems and artworks are like whispers in the quiet night, intertwining shadows and light
within the soul. Each line of verse is a dialogue with myself; each painting is a reflection of
the heart. In the process of creation, I sought freedom in words and found life's rhythm in the
flow of colors.
Gradually, I came to understand that" Woman With No Face" is not about faceless women, but about
every woman whose essence defies superficial definition—her true visage lives in her story and her
breath. May these poems and paintings kindle a gentle glow upon your heart's lake, bringing moments
of peace and resonance.
Thank you for accompanying me on this journey of creation.